SIGHT WORD PHRASES

Written by
Rozanne Lanczak Williams

Editor: Gillian Snoddy
Illustrator: Gloria Jenkins
Cover Illustrator: Holli Conger
Designer/Production: Terri Lamadrid
Art Director: Moonhee Pak
Project Director: Stacey Faulkner

Table of Contents

Sight Word Phrases

Boldface indicates new sight words.

Introduction

Beginning readers build both fluency and comprehension skills when they can read basic sight word vocabulary quickly and automatically. Activities incorporating flash cards, word walls, or word banks have been shown to improve word-recognition skills.

Current research, however, strongly suggests that along with practicing sight words in isolation, repeated readings of sight word phrases and short sentences containing sight words will greatly improve reading fluency and overall reading achievement.* This approach can help avoid word-by-word reading in favor of gaining understanding of written text through fluently reading phrases and short sentences.

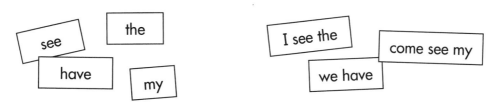

Sight Word Phrases is a flexible resource for helping students build sight word vocabulary in the context of short phrases and sentences. Its unique approach gives students the opportunity to read phrases and short sentences, practice reading and writing sight words as they are introduced, as well as build vocabulary and extend reading practice with user-friendly formats.

WHAT'S INCLUDED:

- A table of contents to easily reference sight word phrases and new sight words being introduced
- 30 phrases containing over 50 of the most common sight words
- 3 activity pages to practice and extend each sight word phrase
- Review pages after every three sets of sight word phrases to provide additional reinforcement and aid retention

The reading skills developed by this resource include:

- Sight word recognition
- Fluent reading of sight word phrases
- Vocabulary development
- Following directions
- Prewriting skills

How to Use the Pages

The sight word phrases activities do not have to be used in any particular order. Select a phrase that fits with your current classroom learning or remedial plan. Use the table of contents to find the phrases you want to use with your students.

Each phrase is introduced, practiced, and extended in three pages. The formats of these pages repeat so students will quickly become familiar and comfortable with the activities. The repetition of the sight word phrases is crucial for helping the brain retain this information.

* Timothy V. Rasinksi, *The Fluent Reader: Oral Reading Strategies for Building Word Recognition, Fluency, and Comprehension*. (New York: Scholastic, 2003), 94.

Sight Word Practice

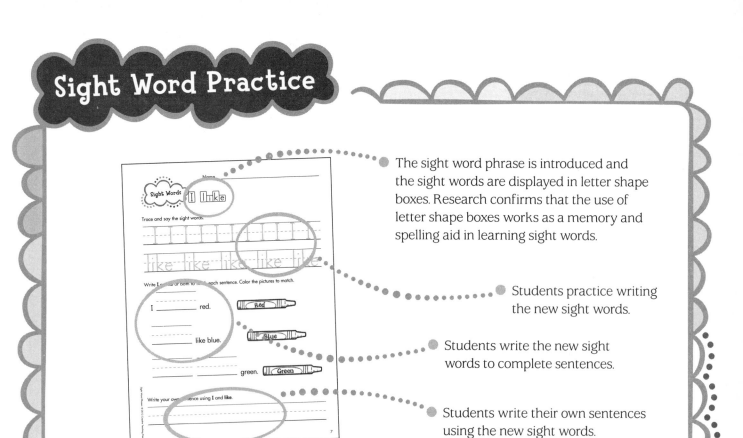

The sight word phrase is introduced and the sight words are displayed in letter shape boxes. Research confirms that the use of letter shape boxes works as a memory and spelling aid in learning sight words.

Students practice writing the new sight words.

Students write the new sight words to complete sentences.

Students write their own sentences using the new sight words.

Vocabulary Practice

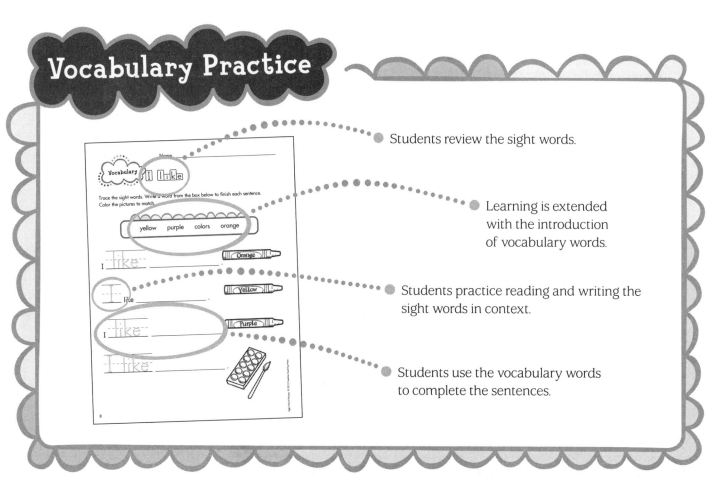

Students review the sight words.

Learning is extended with the introduction of vocabulary words.

Students practice reading and writing the sight words in context.

Students use the vocabulary words to complete the sentences.

Bookmaking Activity

● Students are given an additional opportunity to practice and extend the reading and writing of the sight words, phrases, and short sentences. There are three basic easy-to-make bookmaking activities. See page 6 for the directions on how to make each of the three books.

Review Pages

● Following every three sight word phrases introduced are one or two review pages. These review pages include three formats—a matching page, a fill-in-the-blank page, and a word search puzzle.

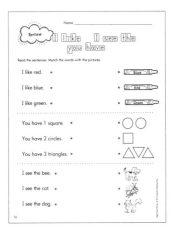

Bookmaking Tips

Each sight word phrase is featured in a bookmaking activity. There are three basic formats, each requiring only one piece of paper. Copy the bookmaking pages on white or colored copy paper or card stock. Students can complete many of the books with their own text and art. Customize the books by adding extra pages or by having students decorate construction paper covers. Flip books can be made sturdier by gluing construction paper or card stock to the back.

DIRECTIONS

The directions are written to the child, in case you would like to send the bookmaking activities home as homework. Copy the directions below and attach them to the bookmaking pages.

FLIP BOOK

1. Finish the book by tracing or writing the words, coloring the pictures, or drawing pictures for blank word cards.
2. Cut out the flip book and the word cards.
3. Staple the word cards to the flip book.
4. "Flip up" each card as you read each sentence or phrase.

STRIP BOOK

1. Finish the book by tracing or writing the words if needed. Draw and color pictures where needed.
2. Cut out the strips.
3. Put the pages in order. Staple them on the left.

FOLD-A-BOOK

1. Finish the book by tracing or writing the words. Draw and color pictures where needed.
2. Cut along the solid lines.
3. Fold the book on the dotted lines to make four pages.

CONNECTING SCHOOL TO HOME

Beginning readers need many opportunities to read and reread familiar text. Provide extra reading practice by sending these books home. Encourage students to store the books in a special "I Can Read Box" at home.

Sight Words I like

Trace and say the sight words.

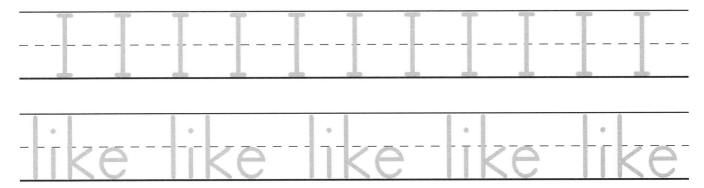

Write **I** or **like** (or both) to finish each sentence. Color the pictures to match.

_____

I _____ red.

_____

_____ like blue.

_____ _____

_____ _____ green.

Write your own sentence using **I** and **like**.

_____

_____

Sight Word Phrases © 2012 Creative Teaching Press

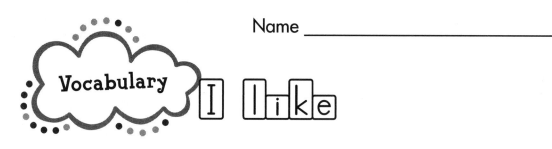

Vocabulary   I like

Trace the sight words. Write a word from the box below to finish each sentence. Color the pictures to match.

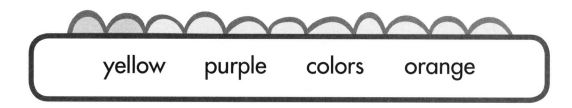

yellow   purple   colors   orange

I _like_ _____ .

Orange

I like _____ .

Yellow

I _like_ _____ .

Purple

I like _____ .

Sight Word Phrases © 2012 Creative Teaching Press

Make a flip book.

Staple word cards here.

red.

I like

orange.

yellow.

green.

blue.

Name _____

Trace and say the new sight words.

you you you you you

have have have have

Write **you** or **have** (or both) to finish each sentence.

You _____ 1 heart.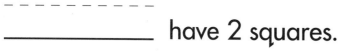

_____ have 2 squares.

_____ _____ 3 rectangles.

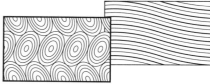 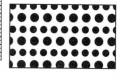

Write your own sentence using **you** and **have**.

_____

_____

Sight Word Phrases © 2012 Creative Teaching Press

Vocabulary

you have

Trace the sight words. Write a word from the box below to finish each sentence.
Draw and color shapes for the last sentence.

shapes   triangles   squares   circles

You _____ have 3 _____ .

You have 5 _____ .

You _____ have 3 _____ .

You have lots of _____ .

Sight Word Phrases © 2012 Creative Teaching Press

Bookmaking

y|ou h|ave

Make a fold-a-book.

3

You have 4 ovals.

2

You have 1 circle.
You have 3 rectangles.

You have 1 butterfly!

4

_____'s

Shapes Book

1

Sight Word Phrases © 2012 Creative Teaching Press

Sight Words I see the

Trace and say the new sight words.

_____

see see see see see

the the the the the

Write **see** or **the** (or both) to finish each sentence.

_____

I see _____ cat.

_____

I _____ the dog.

_____ _____

I _____ _____ monkey.

Write your own sentence using **see** and **the**.

_____

_____

Vocabulary I see the

Trace the sight words. Write a word from the box below to finish each sentence.

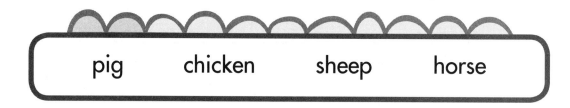

pig   chicken   sheep   horse

I see the _____ .

I _see_ the _____ .

I see _the_ _____ .

I see the _____ .

I see the animals!

14

Sight Word Phrases © 2012 Creative Teaching Press

Bookmaking

 I see the

Make a strip book.

I See the Party

I see the balloons.

1

I see the presents.

2

I see the cake.

3

I see the party!

4

 Review

Name _____

 I like  I see the

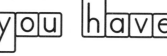 you have

Read the sentences. Match the words with the pictures.

I like red. •

• Blue

I like blue. •

• Red

I like green. •

• Green

You have 1 square. •

• ◯ ◯

You have 2 circles. •

• ☐

You have 3 triangles. •

• △▽△

I see the bee. •

•

I see the cat. •

•

I see the dog. •

•

Sight Word Phrases © 2012 Creative Teaching Press

Name _____

Sight Words

Trace and say the new sight words.

_____

we   we   we   we   we   we

a a a a a a a a a a

Write **we** or **a** (or both) to finish each sentence.

_____

_ _ _ _ _ _ _ _

_____ have a banana.

_____

_ _ _ _ _ _ _

We have _____ carrot.

_____   _____

_ _ _ _ _ _ _   _ _ _ _ _ _ _

_____ have _____ hot dog.

Write your own sentence using **we** and **a**.

_____

_ _

_____

Vocabulary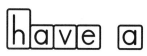

Trace the sight words. Write a word from the box below to finish each sentence.

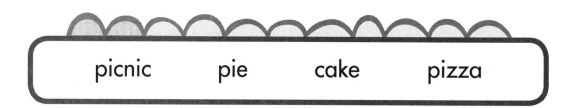

picnic   pie   cake   pizza

We _____ have a _____ .

We have a _____ .

We have a _____ .

We have a _____ .

18

Bookmaking

Make a flip book.

Staple word cards here.

picnic.

We have a

cake.

pizza.

carrot.

banana.

Sight Words

Trace and say the new sight word.

_____

new   new   new   new

Write **new** to finish each sentence.

_____
- - - - - - - - - - - -

We have _____ hats.

_____
- - - - - - - - - - - -

We have _____ T-shirts.

_____
- - - - - - - - - - - -

We have _____ shoes.

Write your own sentence using **new**.

_____

- - - - - - - - - - - - - - - - - -

_____

Sight Word Phrases © 2012 Creative Teaching Press

Vocabulary we have new

Trace the sight words. Write a word from the box below to finish each sentence.

| books | pencils | glue | friends |

We _____ have new _____ .

We _____ have _____ new _____ .

We have _____ new _____ .

We have new _____ .

Name _____

we have new

Make a flip book.

Staple word cards here.

dog!

We have a new

collar.

dish.

toy.

bed.

Sight Word Phrases © 2012 Creative Teaching Press

Name _____

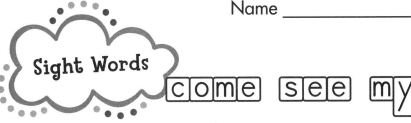

come see my

Trace and say the new sight words.

_____

come come come

_____

my my my my my

Write **come** or **my** (or both) to finish each sentence. Color the bugs.

Come see _____ red bug.

_____ see my green bug.

_____ see _____ brown bug.

Write your own sentence using **come** and **my**.

_____

_____

Vocabulary

come see my

Trace the sight words. Write a word from the box below to finish each sentence. Color the pictures to match the sentences. Draw and color your own picture for the last sentence.

> yellow   purple   black

Come see my _____ bug.

Come see my _____ bug.

Come see my _____ bug.

Come see my bug.

Bookmaking

 come see my

Make a fold-a-book.

3

Come see my _____ bug.

2

Come see my _____ bug.

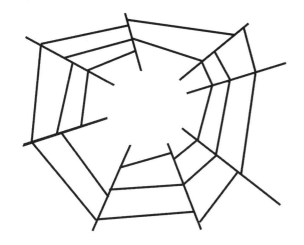

4

Come see my _____ bug.

Come See

_____'s

Bugs!

1

Name _____

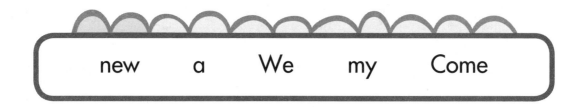

we have a   we have new
come see my

Finish each sentence with a word from the box below. Then read the sentences.

new   a   We   my   Come

1 _____
   _____ have a cake.

2 _____
   _____ see my bug.

3 We have _____ pizza.

4 We have _____ shoes.

5 Come see _____ dog.

26

Name _____

Sight Words

we like to _____ here

Trace and say the new sight words.

to to to to to to to

here here here here

Write **to** or **here** (or both) to finish each sentence.

_____
- - - - - - - - - -
We like _____ read here.

_____
- - - - - - - - - -
We like to paint _____ .

- - - - - - - - - -
We like _____ write _____ .

Write your own sentence using **to** and **here**.

_____
- -
_____

 Name _____

Vocabulary  we like to _____ here

Trace the sight words. Write a word from the box below to finish each sentence. Draw and color your own picture for the last sentence.

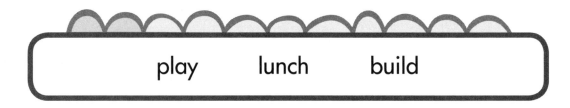

play   lunch   build

We like __to__ _____ here.

We like to eat _____ __here__.

We like __to__ _____ __here__.

Name _____

 **Bookmaking**  we like to _____

Make a fold-a-book.

We like to _____.

3

We like to _____.

2

We like to _____.

4

Here Is What We Like to Do

by _____

1

Sight Word Phrases © 2012 Creative Teaching Press

Sight Words h i s d o g c a n

Trace and say the new sight words.

his his his his his his

can can can can can

Write **his** or **can** to finish each sentence.

_____
- - - - - - - - - -
His dog _____ sit.

_____
- - - - - - -
_____ dog can run.

_____
- - - - - - -
His dog _____ run and play.

Write your own sentence using **his** and **can**.

_____
- -
_____

Vocabulary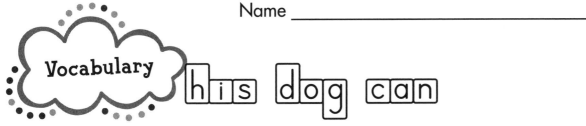

Trace the sight words. Write a word from the box below to finish each sentence.

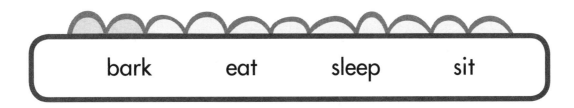

| bark | eat | sleep | sit |

His dog can _____ .

His dog can _____ .

His dog can _____ .

His dog can _____ .

Bookmaking — his dog can

Make a flip book.

	eat
here.	sit
Staple word cards here. / sleep	run
His dog can	hide

Sight Word Phrases © 2012 Creative Teaching Press

Name _____

Trace and say the new sight words.

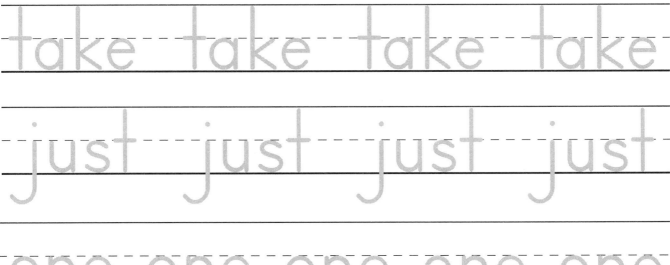

Write **take**, **just**, or **one** to finish each sentence.

You can take just _____ .

You can take _____ one.

You can _____ just one.

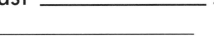

Write your own sentence using **take**, **just**, and **one**.

_____

- -

_____

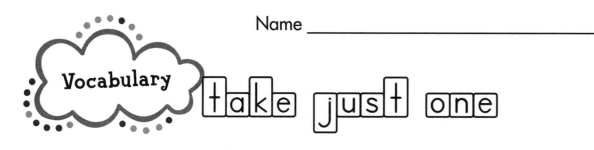

Vocabulary take just one

Trace the sight words. Write a word from the box below to finish each sentence.

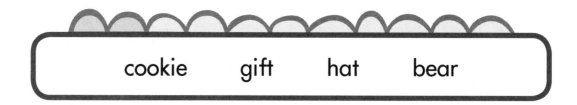

cookie   gift   hat   bear

You can _____take_____ just one _____ .

You can take _____just_____ one _____ .

You can take just _____one_____ _____ .

You can _____take just one_____ _____ .

Name _____

Make a strip book.

Take just one pail.

1

Take just one shovel.

2

Take just one ball.

3

Take just one umbrella.

4

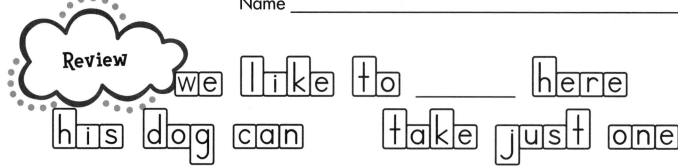

Review

we like to ____ here
his dog can take just one

Read the sentences. Match the words with the pictures.

We like to play here. •

We like to paint here. •

We like to read here. •

His dog can sit. •

His dog can run. •

His dog can eat. •

Take just one hat. •

Take just one bear. •

Take just one cookie. •

Sight Word Phrases © 2012 Creative Teaching Press

Name _____

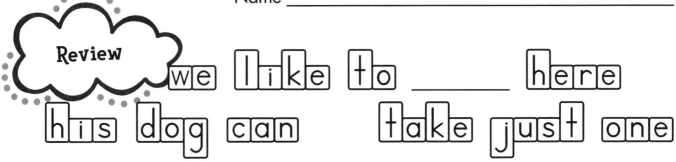

we like to _____ here
his dog can   take just one

Read the words below. Then find and circle them in the puzzle. Words can go → or ↓ .

his	one	here	can
take	just	to	dog

b	r	t	o	p	d
h	i	s	u	h	o
m	t	a	k	e	g
o	p	n	t	r	i
n	c	a	n	e	f
e	g	j	u	s	t

Sight Words l o o k   u p

Trace and say the new sight words.

look look look look

up up up up up up

Write **look** or **up** (or both) to finish each sentence.

Look _____ ! I see a rainbow.

_____ up! I see a plane.

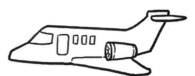

_____ _____ ! I see a bird!

Write your own sentence using **look** and **up**.

_____

_____

Sight Word Phrases © 2012 Creative Teaching Press

Name _____

look up

Trace the sight words. Write a word from the box below to finish each sentence.

| balloon | kite | bird | cloud |

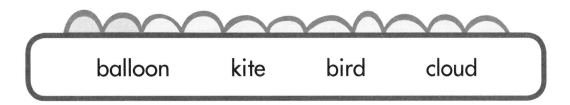

Look up! I see a _____ .

Look _up_ ! I see a _____ .

Look up! I see a _____ .

Look up ! I see a _____ .

Bookmaking look up

Make a fold-a-book.

3

I can see _____.

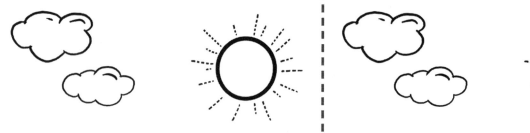

2

I can see a _____.

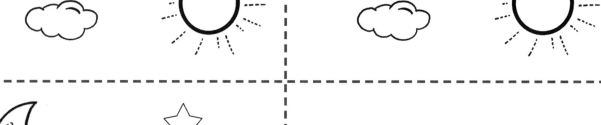

Look Up!

by _____

I can see a _____

and _____.

4

1

Name _____

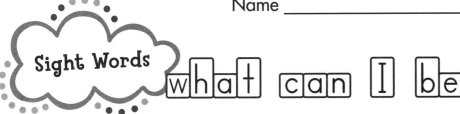

Trace and say the new sight words.

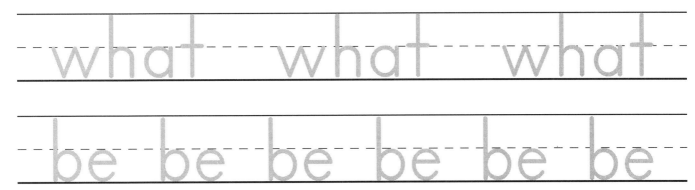

Write **what** or **be** to finish each sentence.

_____

_____ can I be?

I can _____ a doctor.

I can _____ a dancer.

Write your own sentence using **what** and **be**.

_____

_____

Sight Word Phrases © 2012 Creative Teaching Press

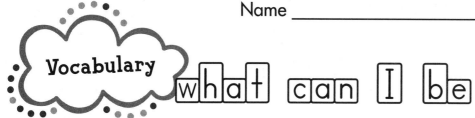

Vocabulary what can I be

Trace the sight words. Write a word from the box below to finish each sentence.

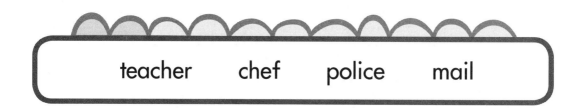

| teacher | chef | police | mail |

What can I be?

I can be a _____ officer.

I _can_ be a _____ .

I can _be_ a _____ carrier.

I can be a _____ .

Sight Word Phrases © 2012 Creative Teaching Press

Name _____

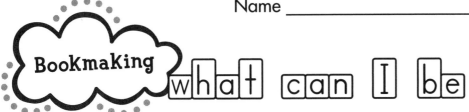

Bookmaking what can I be

Make a strip book.

What Can I Be?

by _____

I can be a dentist.

1

I can be a nurse.

2

I can be a writer.

3

I can be a _____.

4

Sight Words

is on the wall

Trace and say the new sight words.

is is is is is is is is is

on on on on on on

wall wall wall wall

Write **is**, **on**, or **wall** to finish each sentence.

The bird is _____ the wall.

The lizard _____ on the wall.

The frog is on the _____ .

Write your own sentence using **is**, **on**, and **wall**.

_____

Name _____

Trace the sight words. Write a word from the box below to finish each sentence.
Finish the last sentence. Draw a picture to match.

mouse	egg	frog

An _____ is on the wall.

A _____ is on the wall.

A _____ is on the wall.

A _____ is on the wall.

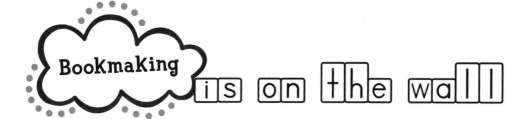
Make a flip book.

Staple word cards here.

A   big egg   is on the wall.

bird   frog   mouse

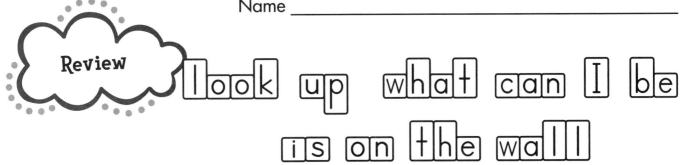

Review

look up what can I be
is on the wall

Finish each sentence with a word from the box below. Then read the sentences.

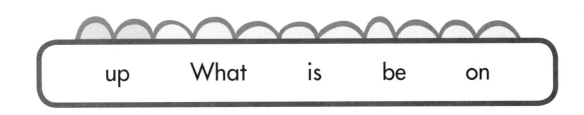

| up | What | is | be | on |

1 _____ can I be?

2 I can _____ a doctor.

3 Look _____ ! It is a plane.

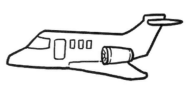

4 A big egg is _____ the wall.

5 A frog _____ on the wall.

Review

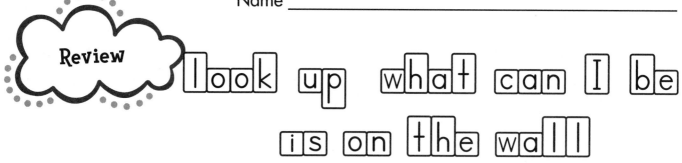

look up what can I be
is on the wall

Read the words below. Then find and circle them in the puzzle. Words can go → or ↓ .

look	up	be	wall
is	what	on	the

t	u	w	h	a	t
u	p	i	c	g	h
i	l	o	o	k	e
s	a	z	n	o	c
w	a	l	l	i	m
b	e	k	s	l	e

48

Sight Word Phrases © 2012 Creative Teaching Press

 **Sight Words**

my cat was in

Trace and say the new sight words.

was was was was

in in in in in in in

Write **was** or **in** (or both) to finish each sentence.

_____

My cat was _____ the tree.

_____

My cat _____ in the box.

_____ _____

My cat _____ _____ the bag.

Write your own sentence using **was** and **in**.

_____

_____

Vocabulary

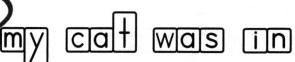

Trace the sight words. Write a word from the box below to finish each sentence.

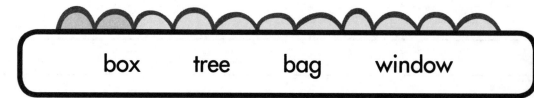

box   tree   bag   window

My cat was in the _____ .

My cat was in the _____ .

My cat was in the _____ .

My cat was in the _____ .

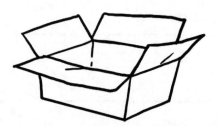

50

Bookmaking

Make a fold-a-book.

3

in the _____.

My _____ was

2

in the _____.

My _____ was

My _____ was

in the _____.

4

Here Is
My Cat

by _____

1

Name _____

Trace and say the new sight word.

this this this this

Write **this** to finish each sentence.

_____

_____ is the jungle.

_____

_____ is the forest.

_____

_____ is the desert.

Write your own sentence using **this**.

_____

_____

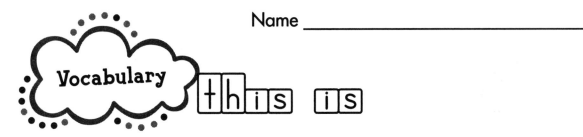 Vocabulary **this is**

Trace the sight words. Write a word from the box below to finish each sentence.

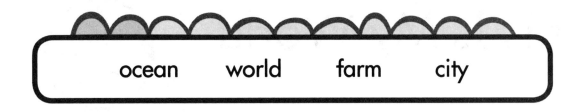

ocean   world   farm   city

This is the _____ .

This is the _____ .

This is the _____ .

This is my _____ !

Make a strip book.

This Is My World

by _____

1

This is my home.

2

This is my school.

3

This is my town.

4

This is my world.

5

Sight Word Phrases © 2012 Creative Teaching Press

 Sight Words 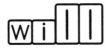 I will _____ with

Trace and say the new sight words.

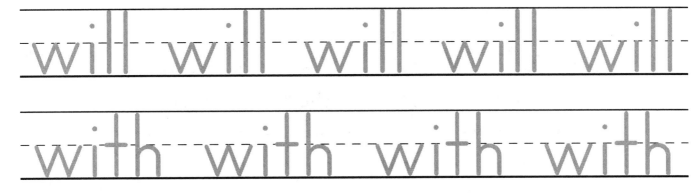

will will will will will

with with with with

Write **will** or **with** (or both) to finish each sentence.

_____

I will run _____ my sister.

_____

I _____ run with my brother.

_____   _____

I _____ run _____ my dog.

Write your own sentence using **will** and **with**.

_____

_____

 Vocabulary

Name _____

I will _____ with

Trace the sight words. Write a word from the box below to finish each sentence.

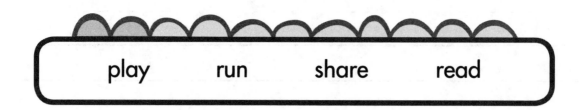

play   run   share   read

I will _____ with my sister.

I will _____ with my mom.

I will _____ with my dad.

I will _____

with my brother.

Sight Word Phrases © 2012 Creative Teaching Press

 I  _____ with

Name _____

Make a flip book.

Staple word cards here.

I will | share | with my _____ .

run | read | paint | play

Name _____

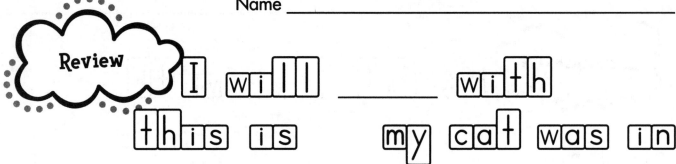

Review

I will _____ with this is my cat was in

Read the sentences. Match the words with the pictures.

My cat was in the grass. ●

My cat was in the box. ●

My cat was in the bag. ●

This is the apple. ●

This is the orange. ●

This is the banana. ●

●

I will run with my brother. ●

I will run with my sister. ●

I will run with my dog. ●

●

●

Sight Word Phrases © 2012 Creative Teaching Press

we are at

Trace and say the new sight words.

are are are are are

at at at at at at at

Write **are** or **at** (or both) to finish each sentence.

_____

We are _____ school.

_____

We _____ at the library.

_____ _____

We _____ _____ music class.

Write your own sentence using **are** and **at**.

_____

_____

Name _____

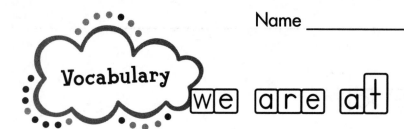
Trace the sight words. Write a word from the box below to finish each sentence.
Draw and color your own picture for the last sentence.

computer   school   lunch   bus

___We___ are at the _____ stop.

We ___are___ at _____ .

We are ___at___ _____ class.

___We are at___ _____!

Name _____

Make a fold-a-book.

ε We are at _____.	ζ We are at _____.
4 We are at _____.	# Where Are We? by _____ 1

Sight Words

get it for

Trace and say the new sight words.

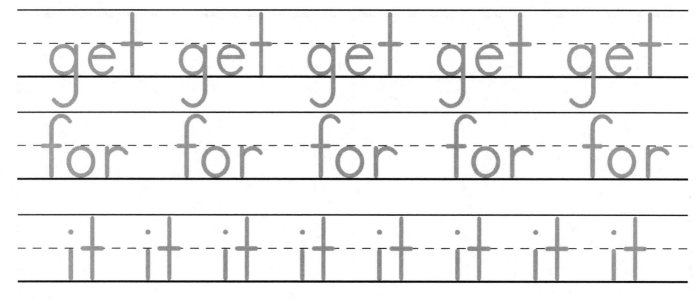

get get get get get

for for for for for

it it it it it it it it

Write **get**, **it**, or **for** to finish each sentence.

Will you get it _____ her?

Will you _____ it for her?

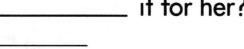

Will you get _____ for her?

Write your own sentence using **get**, **it**, and **for**.

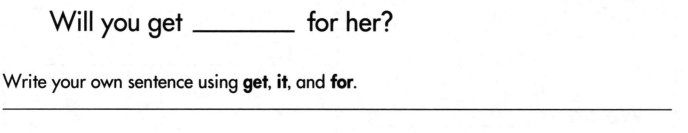

_____

_____

Sight Word Phrases © 2012 Creative Teaching Press

Name _____

Trace the sight words. Write a word from the box below to finish each sentence.

| butter | flour | eggs | sugar |

Will you __get__ the _____ for her?

Will you get the _____ __for__ her?

Will you __get__ the _____ for her?

Will you get the _____ __for__ her?

Then she will bake a cake for you!

Bookmaking — get it for

Make a flip book.

Staple word cards here.

Will you get it for

him?

us?

me?

them?

her?

All About Dogs

Sight Words

we both make

Trace and say the new sight words.

both both both both

make make make

Write **both** or **make** (or both) to finish each sentence.

_____

We _____ are friends.

We both like to _____ cookies.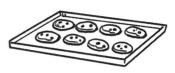

We _____ like to _____ houses.

Write your own sentence using **both** and **make**.

_____

_____

Vocabulary we both make

Trace the sight words. Write a word from the box below to finish each sentence.
Draw and color your own picture for the last sentence.

| cookies | music | ride | cream |

We_____ both like to _____ bikes.

We _both_ like ice _____.

We both _make_ _____.

We both make _____!

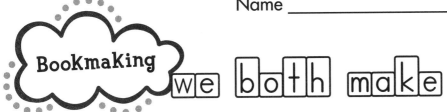

Bookmaking — we both make

Make a strip book.

My Friend

by _____

This is my friend.

1

My friend can make _____.

2

I can make _____.

3

We both make _____.

4

Name _____

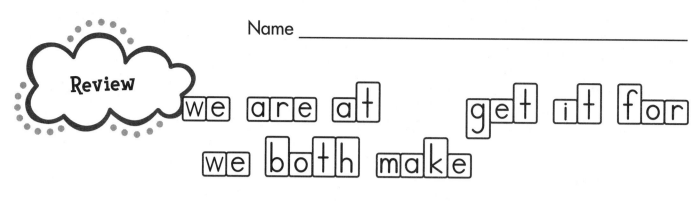

we are at   get it for
we both make

Finish each sentence with a word from the box below. Then read the sentences.

get   are   for   at   make   both

1 We _____ _____ school.

2 I will _____ the book.

3 The cake is _____ her.

4 We _____ make music.

5 We both _____ cookies.

68

Name _____

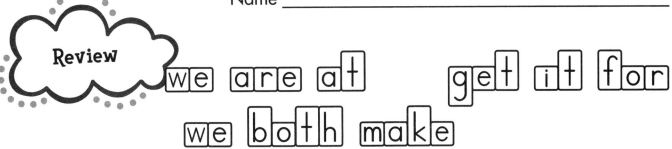

we are at   get it for
we both make

Read the words below. Then find and circle them in the puzzle. Words can go → or ↓ .

for	get	at	like
make	are	both	it

f	o	r	l	s	p
d	a	t	i	u	g
c	m	a	k	e	b
e	h	r	e	j	o
k	i	e	g	e	t
r	t	f	p	i	h

Sight Words
what is your

Trace and say the new sight word.

_____

your your your your

Write **your** to finish each sentence.

_____
What is _____ favorite toy?

_____
What is _____ favorite food?

_____
What is _____ favorite color?

Write your own sentence using **your**.

_____

_____

Name _____

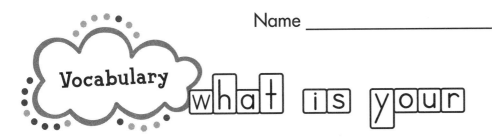

Trace the sight words. Write a word from the box below to finish each sentence.

Draw and color your own picture below each question to show your answer.

> game   animal   color   food

What _____ is your favorite _____?

What is _____ your favorite _____?

Name _____

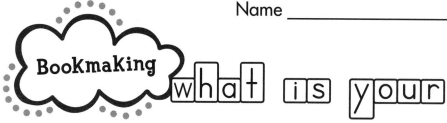

Bookmaking what is your

Make a fold-a-book.

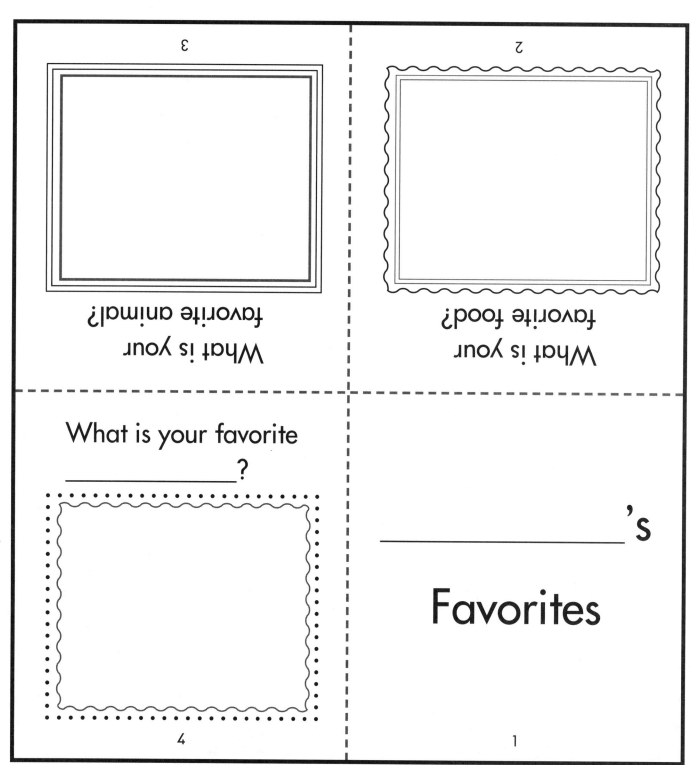

3

What is your
favorite animal?

2

What is your
favorite food?

What is your favorite

_____?

4

_____'s

Favorites

1

Name _____

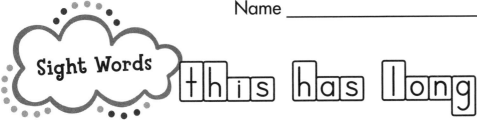

Trace and say the new sight words.

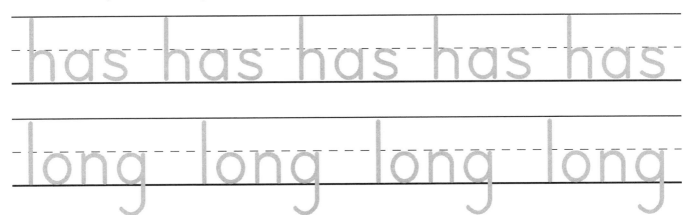

Write **has** or **long** (or both) to finish each sentence.

_____

- - - - - - - - - -

An elephant has a _____ nose.

_____

- - - - - - - - - -

A monkey _____ a long tail.

_____ _____

- - - - - - - - - - - - - - -

This girl _____ _____ hair.

Write your own sentence using **has** and **long**.

_____

- -

_____

Vocabulary  this has long

Trace the sight words. Read and answer each riddle.

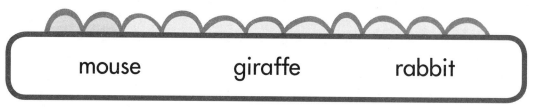

| mouse | giraffe | rabbit |

__This__ has long ears.

It is a _____.

This __has__ a long neck.

It is a _____.

This has a __long__ tail.

It is a _____.

Name ______________________________

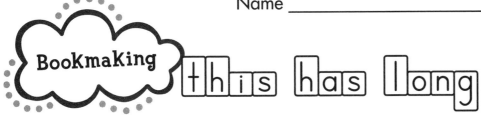

BooKmaKing

this has long

Make a fold-a-book.

What Is This?

by ____________________

1

This is black.

This has 8 long legs.

This is a ____________.

2

This is gray.

This has 2 long tusks.

This is a/an ____________.

3

This is ____________.

This has ____________.

This is a ____________.

4

Sight Words they were

Trace and say the new sight words.

they they they they

were were were

Write **they** or **were** (or both) to finish each sentence.

They _____ jumping.

_____ were in the mud.

_____ _____ in the tub.

Write your own sentence using **they** and **were**.

_____

_____

Vocabulary they were

Trace the sight words. Write a word from the box below to finish each sentence.
Draw and color your own picture for the last sentence.

jumping	making	going

They were _____ up the hill.

They were _____ .

They were _____ mud pies.

Sight Word Phrases © 2012 Creative Teaching Press

Bookmaking they were

Make a strip book.

Monsters

by _____

1

They were _____.

2

They were _____.

3

They were _____.

4

Sight Word Phrases © 2012 Creative Teaching Press

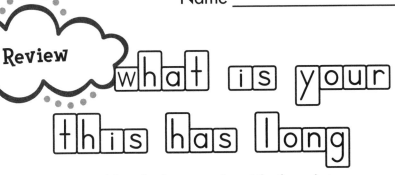

Read the sentences. Match the words with the pictures.

What is your favorite food? •

What is your favorite toy? •

What is your favorite book? •

The mouse has a long tail. •

The monkey has a long tail. •

The cat has a long tail. •

They were jumping. •

They were going up. •

They were making mud pies. •

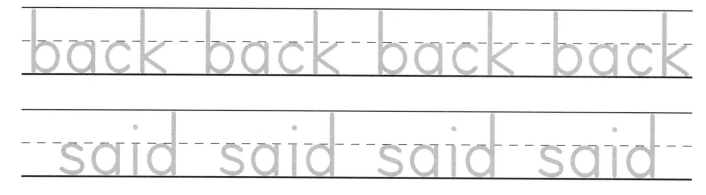

" Come back," said _____ .

Trace and say the new sight words.

back back back back

said said said said

Write **back** or **said** to finish each sentence.

The cookie ran and ran.

_____

_____

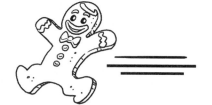

"Come back!" _____ the pig.

_____

"Come _____ !" said the cow.

Write your own sentence using **back** and **said**.

_____

_____

Vocabulary "Come back," said _____.

Trace the sight words. Write a word from the box below to finish each sentence.

girl	wolf	pigs

" _____

__Come__ back!"

said the _____.

....

"Come __back__!"

said the _____.

....

"Come back!" __said__

the _____.

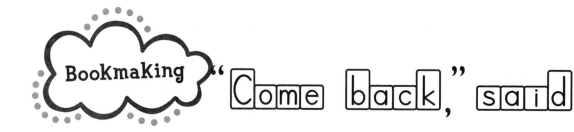

Bookmaking "Come back," said _____.

Make a flip book.

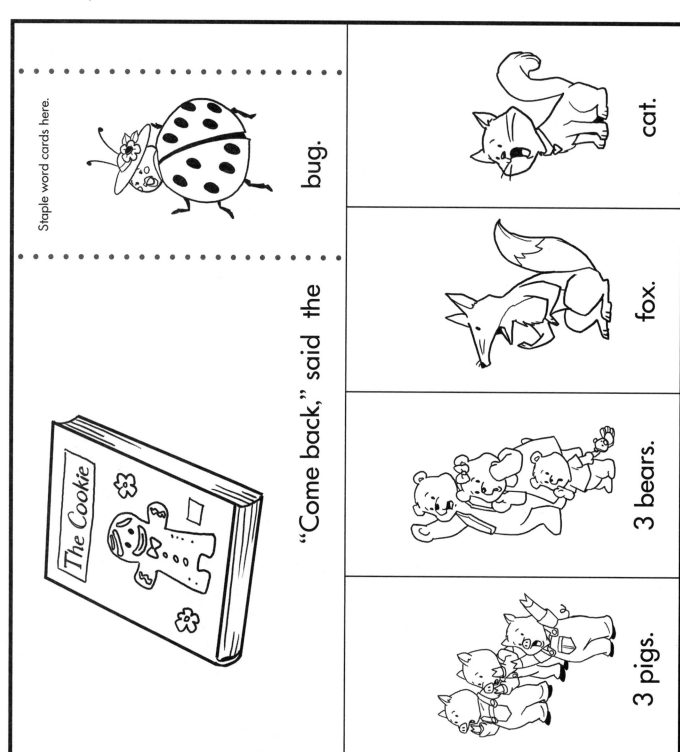

Sight Word Phrases © 2012 Creative Teaching Press

Sight Words

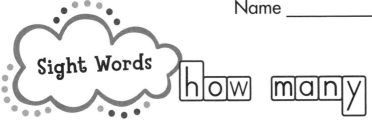

Trace and say the new sight words.

how how how how

many many many

Write **how** or **many** (or both) to finish each sentence.

_____

How _____ bees do you see?

_____

_____ many spiders do you see?

_____ _____

bugs do you see?

Write your own sentence using **how** and **many**.

_____

_____

 **Vocabulary** how many

Name _____

Trace the sight words. Write a word from the box below to finish each sentence. Read and answer each riddle.

leaf   grass   wall

<u>How</u> many spiders

are on the _____?

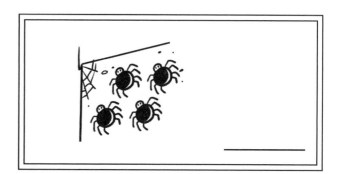

How <u>many</u> caterpillars

are on the _____?

<u>How many</u>

ants are in the _____?

Sight Word Phrases © 2012 Creative Teaching Press

Name _____

Bookmaking how many

Make a fold-a-book.

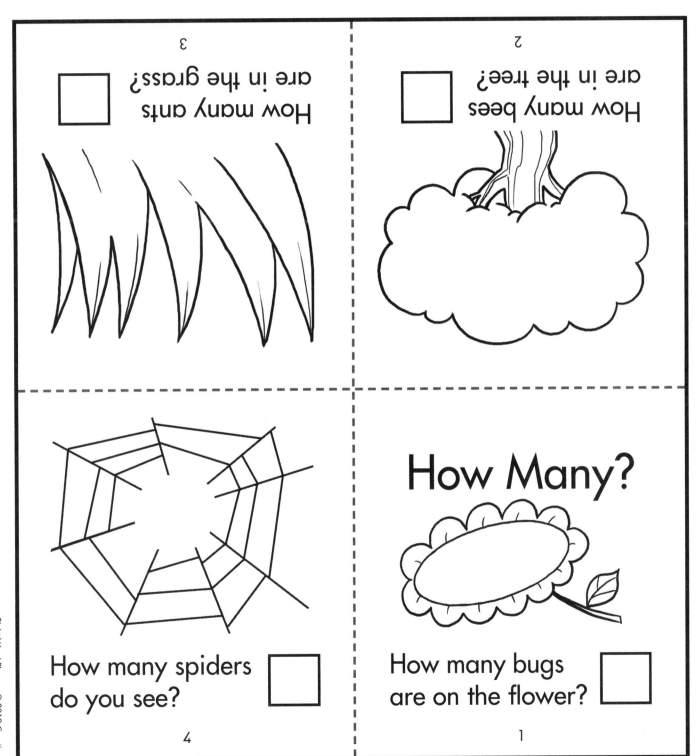

3

How many ants
are in the grass?

□

2

How many bees
are in the tree?

□

How many spiders
do you see?

□

4

How Many?

How many bugs
are on the flower?

□

1

Name _____

 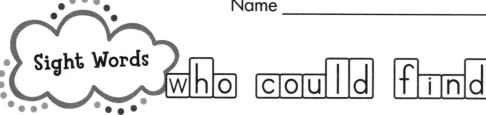

Trace and say the new sight words.

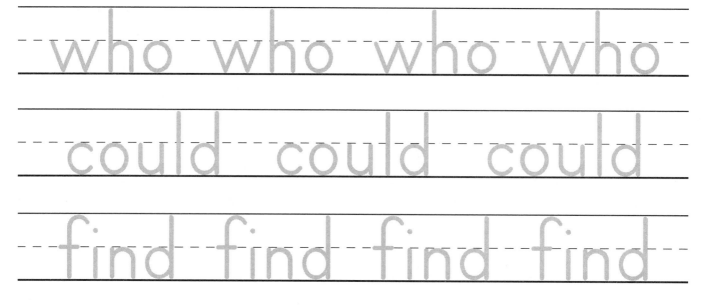

Write **who**, **could**, or **find** to finish each sentence.

_____
- - - - - - - - - - - - - - -
Who could _____ onions?

_____
- - - - - - - - - - - - - - -
Who _____ find beans?

_____
- - - - - - - - - - - - - - -
_____ could find potatoes?

Write your own sentence using **who**, **could**, and **find**.

_____
- -
_____

86

Name _____

Trace the sight words. Write a word from the box below to finish each sentence.

| carrots | corn | tomatoes |

" _____Who_____ could find some _____ ?"

asked Little Red Hen.

"Who _____could_____ find some

_____ ?" asked Little Red Hen.

" _____Who could find_____ some

_____ ?" asked Little Red Hen.

Name _____

 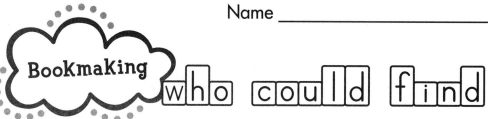
Make a strip book.

"I could put in the carrots,"
said Rabbit.

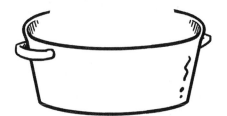

1

"I could put in the green beans,"
said Duck.

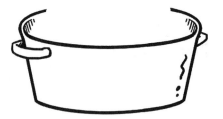

2

"I could put in the potatoes,"
said Dog.

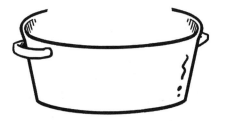

3

Mmm! Yummy vegetable soup!

4

Sight Word Phrases © 2012 Creative Teaching Press

Name _____

"Come back," said _____.
how many   who could find

Finish each sentence with a word from the box below. Then read the sentences.

Who   How   back   could   said   find   many

1 "Come _____ !" said the pigs.

2 "Come back!" _____ the bears.

3 Who _____ find some beans?

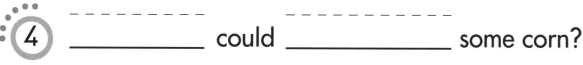 

4 _____ could _____ some corn?

5 _____ _____ bugs do you see?

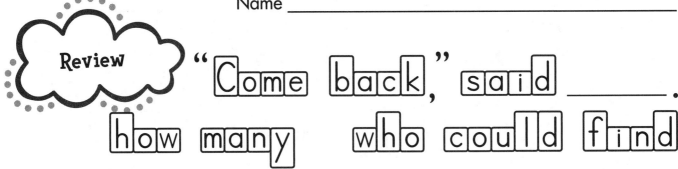

Review "Come back," said _____.
how many who could find

Read the words below. Then find and circle them in the puzzle. Words can go → or ↓.

who	back	said	many
how	could	find	come

d	r	h	s	p	u
c	c	o	u	l	d
o	b	w	r	o	s
m	a	n	y	b	a
e	c	w	h	o	i
t	k	f	i	n	d

Name _____

where have you been

Trace and say the new sight words.

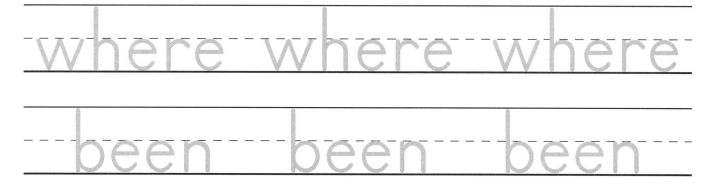

where where where

been been been

Write **where** or **been** (or both) to finish each sentence.

_____

_____ have you been?

Where have you _____ ?

_____   _____

_____ have you _____ ?

Write your own sentence using **where** and **been**.

_____

_____

Name _____

where have you been

Trace the sight words. Write a word from the box below to finish each sentence.

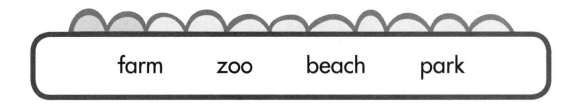

farm   zoo   beach   park

Where have you been ?

I _have_ been to the _____.

I have _been_ to the _____.

I _have_ been to the _____.

I have _been_ to the _____.

Name _____

Make a flip book.

Staple word cards here.

Where have you been?

We have been to the

museum.

nature center.

zoo.

farm.

 Sight Words

Trace and say the new sight words.

which which which

way way way way

did did did did did

go go go go go go

Write **which**, **way**, **did**, or **go** to finish the sentences.

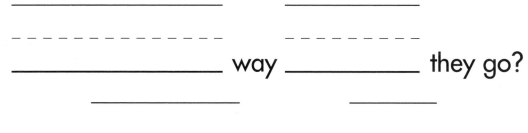

_____ way _____ they go?

Which _____ did they _____ ?

THIS WAY

THAT WAY

Write your own sentence using **which**, **way**, **did**, and **go**.

_____

- -

Sight Word Phrases © 2012 Creative Teaching Press

Vocabulary

Trace the sight words. Write a word from the box below to finish each sentence.

fish   cat   frog   bird

Which _____ way did the _____ go?

Which way did the _____ go?

Which way did the _____ go?

Which way did the _____ go ?

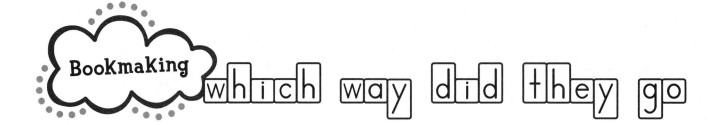

which way did they go

Make a fold-a-book.

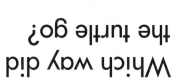

3

Which way did
the turtle go?

FINISH

2

Which way did
the frog go?

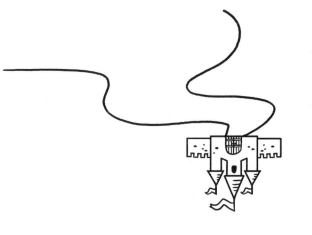

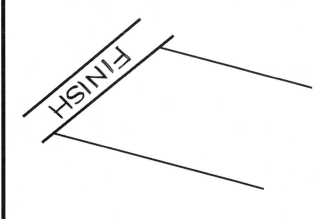

Which way did
the 3 kittens go?

4

Which Way
Did They Go?

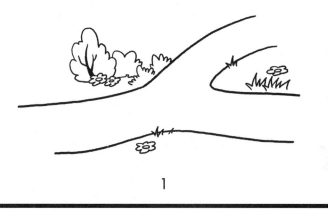

1

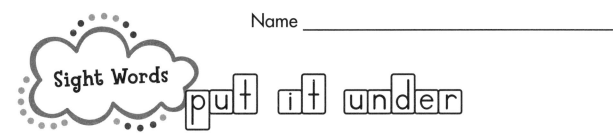

Sight Words

put it under

Trace and say the new sight words.

put put put put put

under under under

Write **put** or **under** (or both) to finish each sentence.

_____

I put it _____ my pillow.

_____

I _____ it under my pillow.

_____   _____

I _____ it _____ my pillow.

Write your own sentence using **put** and **under**.

_____

_____

Sight Word Phrases © 2012 Creative Teaching Press

Vocabulary put it under

Trace the sight words. Write a word from the box below to finish each sentence.

tree	bed	table	plate

I __put__ it under my _____.

I put __it__ under my _____.

I put it __under__ the _____.

I __put it under__ _____

the _____.

Sight Word Phrases © 2012 Creative Teaching Press

Bookmaking

put it under

Make a flip book.

under my bed.

it

I put

Staple word cards here.

my ____

my ____

that

this

Name _____

where have you been
which way did they go
put it under

Read the sentences. Match the words with the pictures.

We have been to the park. •

We have been to the zoo. •

We have been to the farm. •

Which way did the 3 pigs go? •

Which way did the turtle go? •

Which way did the frog go? •

I put it under my pillow. •

I put it under my bed. •

I put it under my plate. •

Sight Word Phrases © 2012 Creative Teaching Press

Review where have you been which way did they go put it under

Read the words below. Then find and circle them in the puzzle. Words can go → or ↓.

put	way	which	under
where	go	been	did

o	w	h	i	c	h	g
s	w	a	y	p	n	x
g	o	s	k	u	w	a
o	t	v	f	t	h	y
c	h	u	n	d	e	r
b	e	e	n	i	r	z
g	y	z	i	d	e	l

Name _____

 I know how to

Trace and say the new sight word.

know   know   know

Write **know** to finish each sentence.

I _____ how to read.

I _____ how to write.

I _____ how to jump rope.

I _____ how to add.

Write your own sentence using **know**.

_____

- - - - - - - - - - - - - - - - - -

_____

 Vocabulary

 I know how to

Trace the sight words. Write a word from the box below to finish each sentence.

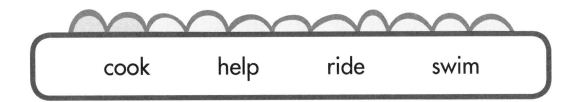

| cook | help | ride | swim |

I know how to _____ my bike.

I _know_ how to _____ .

I know _how_ to _____ .

I know how _to_ _____ .

Bookmaking — I know how to

Make a fold-a-book.

3

• _____

_____

_____ I know how to

2

• _____

_____

_____ I know how to

I know how to _____

_____

_____

_____ •

4

What I Know

by _____

1

Sight Word Phrases © 2012 Creative Teaching Press

Sight Words

these are from me

Trace and say the new sight words.

these these these

from from from

me me me me me

Write **these**, **from**, or **me** to finish each sentence.

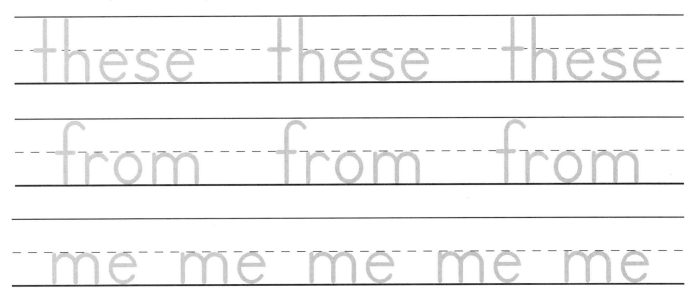

_____

These are _____ me to you.

_____

_____ are from me to you.

_____

These are from _____ to you.

Write your own sentence using **these**, **from**, and **me**.

_____

_____

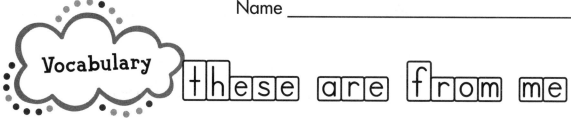

Vocabulary **these are from me**

Trace the sight words. Write a word from the box below to finish each sentence.

| market | bakery | teacher | library |

_____
These are from the _____.

_____
These **are** from the _____.

_____
These are **from** the _____.

_____
These are from

my _____ !

Sight Word Phrases © 2012 Creative Teaching Press

Name _____

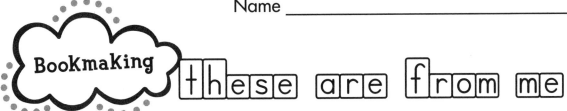

Bookmaking these are from me

Make a strip book.

From Me

by _____

1

These are from me

to _____.

2

These are from me

to _____.

3

These are from me

to _____.

4

Name _____

Trace and say the new sight words.

want   want   want

there   there   there

Write **want** or **there** (or both) to finish each sentence.

_____

We want to sleep _____ .

_____

We _____ to sleep there.

_____   _____

We _____ to sleep _____ .

Write your own sentence using **want** and **there**.

_____

_____

108

Name _____

Vocabulary

 We want to _____ there

Trace the sight words. Write a word from the box below to finish each sentence.

swim   sleep   hike   eat

We _____ want to _____ there.

We want _____ to _____ there.

We want to _____ _____ there.

We want to _____ there.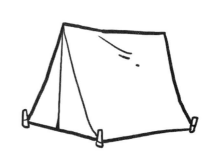

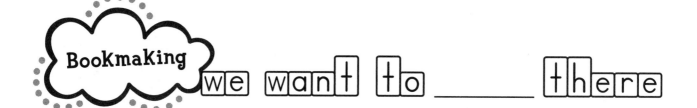

Bookmaking

we want to _____ there

Make a flip book.

Staple word cards here.

We want to

eat

there.

swim

read

play

Name _____

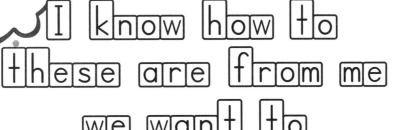

Finish each sentence with a word from the box below. Then read the sentences.

| from | These | want | know | there |

1 I _____ to help.

2 We want to go _____.

3 These are _____ me.

4 _____ are from her.

5 I _____ how to read!

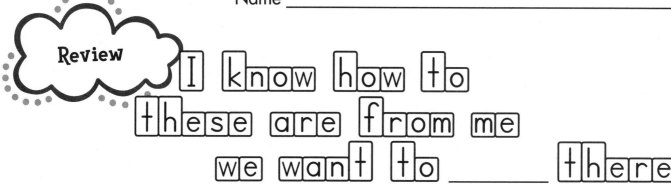

Review

I know how to
these are from me
we want to _____ there

Read the words below. Then find and circle them in the puzzle. Words can go → or ↓.

know	these	want	there	from	me

t	x	i	k	t	e	t
h	x	k	n	f	i	h
e	f	n	v	z	m	e
r	r	o	c	k	f	s
e	o	w	j	n	w	e
d	m	y	a	d	v	u
e	w	a	n	t	f	a